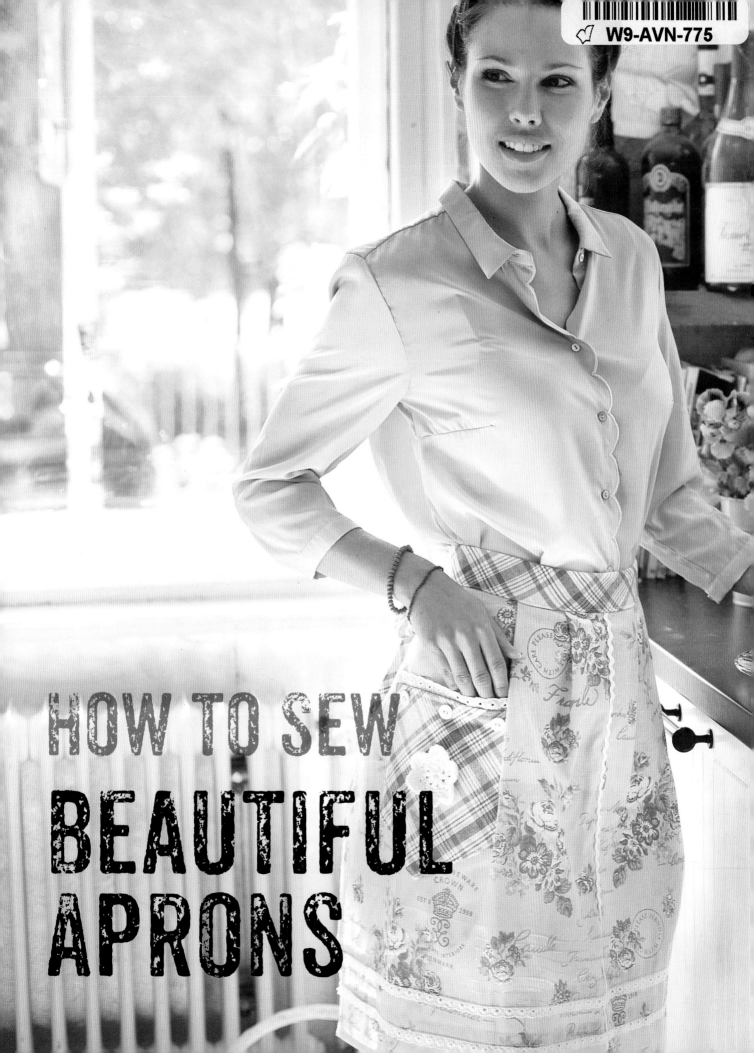

HOW TO SEW
BEAUTIFUL
APRONS

HOW TO SEW
BEAUTIFUL
APRONS

Christa Rolf

SEARCH PRESS

First published in Great Britain 2015
by Search Press Limited
Wellwood, North Farm Road,
Tunbridge Wells, Kent TN2 3DR

Original edition © 2013
World rights reserved by Oz-Verlag-GmbH,
Rheinfelden/Germany

Originally published in Germany as
Meine Nähmode

Text copyright © Christa Rolf 2013

Photographs by Sophie Jendreyko
and Paul Bricknell
Styling by Julia Quante
Hair and make-up styling by
Malina Nithack
Styling assistants: Cinta Villapadiema
and Ha Phan Bich
Models: Prescilla & Katharina (Modelwerk)

ISBN: 978-1-78221-151-8

The Publishers and author can accept no
responsibility for any consequences arising from
the information, advice or instructions given in
this publication.

Suppliers
For details of suppliers, please visit the Search
Press website: www.searchpress.com.

Printed in China

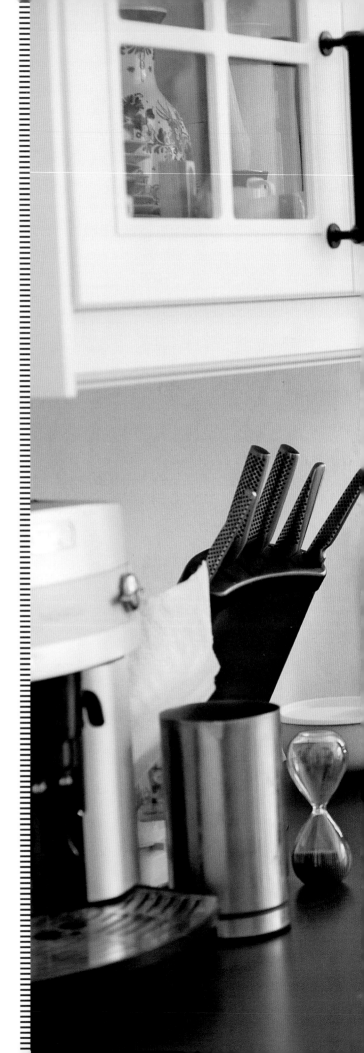

CONTENTS

Introduction 8

Materials & equipment 10

Basic techniques 12

The projects 14

Nordic Inspiration,
page 14

Flowers & Frills,
page 16

Rosy Waist Apron,
page 18

Upcycled,
page 30

Tea Time,
page 32

Romantic Roses,
page 34

Good Enough to Eat
page 46

Polka Dots & Stripes,
page 48

One for the Boys,
page 50

Pippi Longstocking Apron,
page 52

Budding Bakers,
page 20

Gardening Apron,
page 22

Tea Towel Apron,
page 24

Fairy Apron,
page 26

Taste of Tradition,
page 28

Masterchefs,
page 36

Spick & Span,
page 38

Dirndl Apron,
page 40

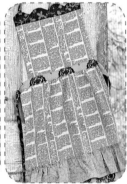

Newsprint Apron,
page 42

Smartly Ruffled,
page 44

From the Heart,
page 54

Sweet Temptation,
page 56

Neon Bright,
page 58

Owl Apron,
page 60

The Two of Us,
page 62

INTRODUCTION

Aprons remain wonderfully practical accessories with an undeniably nostalgic charm about them. They remind us of our childhood when baking cakes and helping our mothers and fathers around the home were new and exciting experiences. This book aims to recapture this feeling of domestic nostalgia for a whole new generation. With these simple but inventive projects you can share new and precious moments with your own families.

There are twenty-five designs in a range of colours and styles, including several options for children. Choose from pretty, simple styles or opt for a more kitsch or 'upcycled' look. Alternatively, there are brighter designs in neon colours as well as the traditional 'dirndl' style aprons from Germany and many designs with more practical features for baking and working in the garden.

All the aprons can be sewn by hand and most of the projects are suitable for the absolute beginner. To help you get started, you will find some basic sewing instructions at the beginning of the book as well as full-size pattern templates for the projects at the back.

My warmest thanks go to all the creative designers who provided their patterns and ideas for this delightful book.

Happy sewing!

Christa Rolf

NOTE:

In projects where only the fabric length measurement is given, the width is assumed to be a standard fabric roll width of either 115cm (44–45in) or 150cm (58–60in.)

MATERIALS & EQUIPMENT

Aprons make simple sewing projects and you will only require the most basic of sewing materials to get started.

Sewing machine: you'll need a reliable sewing machine with a straight stitch and some embroidery stitches for decoration.

Threads: make sure you have a wide variety of sewing and embroidery threads at your disposal as well as cotton yarns for embellishing your projects.

Steam iron: a good steam iron is essential when working with fabric.

Fabrics: you will need a good stash of cotton or polyester fabrics in a variety of patterns. Some of the projects require you to use leftover materials from old clothes and to 'upcycle' fabrics.

Hand-sewing needles: make sure you have a good selection of needles in a range of sizes that will suit different thicknesses of fabric and thread.

Buttons: a few of these aprons require the odd button for embellishment. It is always useful to have a few sets of matching buttons on hand along with your fabric stash.

Scissors: a sharp pair of fabric scissors is essential. You may also find that a good pair of pinking shears will come in handy to give a decorative edge to your fabrics and to stop them from fraying.

Pins: you will need a good selection of pins to hold your fabrics in place. A magnetic pin holder is a helpful tool for holding all your pins – or, failing that, a pincushion.

Tape measure: make sure you have one of these to accurately measure the fabrics for each project.

Seam ripper: it is often useful to have a seam ripper on hand for any sewing mistakes or to salvage fabric from old clothes.

Water-soluble pen: use one of these for marking out template patterns on fabric or, alternatively, you can use chalk or a chalk wheel.

Point turner: this is an optional, but helpful little tool that you can use to create sharp, professional-looking corners in your projects when turning through.

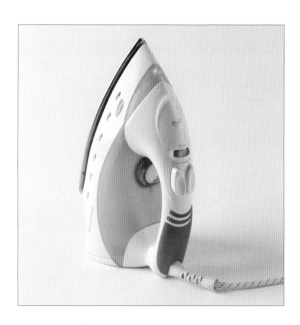

Clockwise from top left: pinking shears, dressmaking scissors, embroidery scissors, pins and magnetic holder, pincushion, hand-sewing needles, water-soluble pen, point turner, chalk pencils, chalk wheel, tape measure and seam ripper.

BASIC TECHNIQUES

MAKING STRAPS, WAIST TIES AND LOOPS

This is one way to make aprons straps (some projects use slightly different methods). Fold the fabric strips in half, lengthways, with the wrong sides facing and iron. Open out and fold the two long sides over to the middle crease you have just created and iron. Invert the folded strip folding it so that the long edges now meet with right sides facing. Edge stitch the strip along the long edge and ends leaving a small gap for turning through. Turn through and sew the gap closed by hand and iron again.

SEWING A YO-YO

Fabric yo-yos make great optional extras for embellishing your aprons. To make one, cut out a fabric circle twice the size of your desired yo-yo. Fold the fabric edge over to the wrong side by 5mm (¼in), and insert a needle. Start making small, vertical folds along the edge of your folded fabric with small, consistent intervals between each vertical fold. Sew through the folds with a double thread in a matching colour. When you have sewn all the way around the circumference, tighten the thread so that the circle is drawn together. Knot the ends of the thread and secure.

GATHERING

To achieve gathered edges, loosen the top tension on your sewing machine and set the longest stitch length. Sew two parallel lines 5mm (¼in) apart; do not secure. These two sewn lines will be right and left of the later seam. Carefully pull the two loose threads until the fabric is the desired width, and make sure the gathers are even over the entire line. The gathered thread, which is still visible, can be removed when finished.

TURNING RIGHT SIDE OUT

Place two pieces of fabric together, right sides facing, and sew together around the edges at a presser foot's distance. Leave a small section open through which to turn the fabric right side out. Secure the beginning and end of the stitching. Trim the seam allowances (except at the turning opening) leaving between 2mm ($^{1}/_{10}$ in) for small items and 5mm (¼in) for large items. Cut across the points on the outer corners, and trim the inner corners and curves to just before the seam. Turn the item right side out, and carefully push out the corners. Sew up the opening by hand.

USING VOLUME FLEECE OR WADDING/BATTING

A layer of fleece is placed between two fabric layers and is either pinned or ironed before they are sewn together.

BACKSTITCH

This stitch, which is worked from right to left, is ideal for tight corners and curves. Pull the needle through at point 'a'. Move it along a little to the right and insert at point 'b', then draw it out again at point 'c'. Return to point 'a', and insert the needle again. Repeat, drawing the thread through after every stitch.

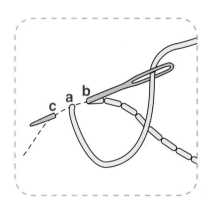

SATIN STITCH

This stitch is ideal for filling areas: it is a little like colouring in. With smaller motifs, run the stitches over the entire area that is to be filled; for larger ones, allow the stitches to run into each other. Pull the needle through on the pattern line and insert it again on the opposite side. Run the thread under the fabric, and bring it through again right next to the previous stitch. Continue like this until you have filled the entire area with close stitches.

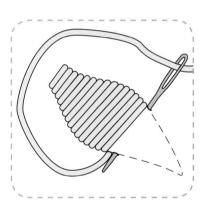

STAR STITCH

To make small stars, simply sew three basic satin stitches on top of each other in the shape of a star. Sew six satin stitches for bigger stars, working from the outside to the middle of the star.

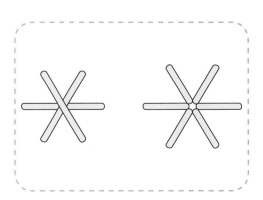

NORDIC
INSPIRATION

by Christa Rolf

Measurements **75 x 70cm (29½ x 27½in)**
Templates **Pattern sheet A**

Materials

25 x 100cm (9¾ x 39½in) pink and white polka
dot fabric
25 x 140cm (9¾ x 55in) pink and white striped fabric
20 x 75cm (7¾ x 29½in) pink and white checked fabric
fabric scraps in pink patterns
15 x 15cm (6 x 6in) fusible webbing
20cm (7¾in) narrow rickrack braid in pink and white
20cm (7¾in) wide rickrack braid in white
2 white buttons
white and dark blue embroidery yarn
2 old pairs of jeans
sewing cotton
water-soluble marker pen

Cutting out

The pattern templates include a 1cm (½in)
seam allowance.

Pink and white polka dot fabric:
10 x 85cm (4 x 33½in) (strap)

Pink and white striped fabric:
2 pieces 12 x 120cm
(4¾ x 47¼in) (waist ties)

Pink and white checked fabric:
16 x 74cm (3¼ x 29¼in) cut against the bias
(hem binding)

SEWING

1 To make the apron, cut one of the legs off one pair of jeans. Cut open the inside seam and trim neatly. Zigzag over the long raw edges to neaten. Fold over to the wrong side by about 1cm (½in) and tack around all edges.

2 To make the bottom hem, take the checked fabric and start by following the instructions for 'Making straps' on page 12, however, rather than edge stitching the strip, unfold it and pin your fabric strip flush to the lower hem so that they are right sides facing and the edge of the strip is 2cm (¾in) from the bottom edge of the apron. The hem should be 2cm (¾in) longer than the apron at both ends. Sew the strip in place along the front and then fold the hem into position folding the back seam of the hem to the back of the apron. The back seam of your hem should have the raw edge folded inwards so that you can conceal the folded edge flush against the back of your piece, creating a neat finish and hiding the raw edge. Sew in place, then fold the overhanging edges of the hem to the back and hand stitch them in place.

3 For the appliqué pieces, transfer the pennant pattern piece to the fusible webbing five times and cut out. Iron the fusible webbing shapes onto the back of five different fabrics, then cut them out along the drawn line. Next, use the water-soluble marker pen to draw an arched line on the apron to mark where your line of bunting will appear. Sew the white embroidery yarn onto the drawn line using a tiny zigzag stitch. Place the pennants on the line and iron on. Secure 2mm (¹/₁₀in) from the outer edges of the motifs in dark blue yarn. Double stitch to make the line more clearly visible.

4 To make the waist ties, take the striped fabric and follow the instructions for 'Making straps' on page 12. Align your waist ties on either end of your apron and sew the ends in place to attach.

5 To make the neck strap, take the polka dot fabric and follow the instructions for 'Making straps' on page 12. Next, push each end of the strap under the jeans hem at the top of your apron and sew in place. Sew a button into the middle of each seam on the front of the apron.

6 Use two pockets from the second pair of jeans to make the patch pockets. Sew two pieces of the narrow rickrack braid in pink and white onto one of the pockets. For the other pocket, make the boat and sail appliqué pieces from the templates and position as shown. Sew all around the boat 2mm (¹/₁₀in) from the edge. Sew back and forth several times to make the mast, attaching the short side of the sail as you go. Place the wide rickrack braid over the bottom of the boat and sew on. Sew both the pockets to the apron to finish.

FLOWERS & FRILLS

by Steffie Geppert

Measurements **75 x 70cm (29½ x 27½in)**
Templates **Pattern sheet A**

Materials

70 x 140cm (27½ x 55in) light blue floral fabric
65 x 160cm (25½ x 63in) light green fabric
45 x 160cm (17¾ x 63in) pink checked fabric
20 x 150cm (7¾ x 59in) white fabric with blue spots
scraps of green and white checked fabric
scrap of pink felt
10cm (4in) fusible webbing
matching thread
2 flowers cut from the blue floral fabric
20cm (7¾in) pink satin ribbon, 2mm (¹/₁₀in) wide

Cutting out

A seam allowance of 7.5mm (³/₈in) is included in the measurements. The pattern pieces contain no seam allowance.

Light blue floral fabric:
2 apron pattern pieces on the fold line

Light green fabric:
2 bib pattern pieces on the fold line
1 pocket pattern piece on the fold line
2 strips 6 x 136cm (2¼ x 53½in) (hem frill)

Pink checked fabric:
1 strip 5 x 88cm (2 x 34¾in) (top frill)
6 diagonal strips, 4cm (1½in) wide (binding)

White fabric with blue spots:
4 pieces 6 x 30cm (2¼ x 11¾in) (straps)
4 pieces 5 x 64cm (2 x 25¼in) (waist ties)

PREPARATION

1 Transfer all the pattern templates to the wrong side of their respective fabrics and cut out. Be sure to include the darts on the bib pattern template.

2 For the straps and waist ties, place two pieces of white fabric with blue spots together with the right sides facing. Use the diagram accompanying the templates to draw on a point on each of the short sides. The length of the point for the straps is 12cm (4¾in), and the point on the waist ties should be 4cm (1½in).

3 For the binding, sew together the diagonal strips of pink checked fabric into one long strip.

4 For the appliqué, transfer the oval and zigzag oval pattern pieces to the fusible webbing and cut out. Iron the oval onto the back of the scraps of green and white checked fabric and the zigzag oval onto the back of the pink felt and cut out.

5 To embroider the text, transfer the words 'Sweet tooth' to the green and white checked fabric and backstitch along the drawn line. Fill in with satin stitch.

6 Remove the backing paper from the oval, then iron it onto the middle of the pink felt piece.

SEWING

1 Fold over the straps and waist ties (see Basic techniques, page 12), leaving the straight short side open for turning. Edge stitch on all sides.

2 Bind the pocket by pinning the diagonal pink strip to the edges with right sides facing, cut to the right length and sew. Fold the strip 1cm (½in) over the edges and edge stitch. Place the pocket in the middle of the blue floral apron piece 17cm (6¾in) from the top, and sew along the bottom edge. Sew on the flowers cut from the fabric and attach the satin ribbon to the pocket for decoration.

3 For the hem frill, sew the light green fabric strips together to make one long strip. Fold over then iron one long side and the two short sides by 1cm (½in) to the wrong side, and secure with zigzag stitch. Gather the raw long edge to a length of 142cm (56in) (see Basic techniques, page 12). Work the top frill in the same way, but gather this one to 42cm (16½in).

4 Fold the apron piece together along the fold line, right sides facing, and put the green hem frill between them along the bottom edge with the frill facing inside. Sew together and turn over. For the bib, close up the darts by folding the piece, right sides facing, along the middle of the dart, and sew together along the drawn line.

5 Remove the backing paper from the felt appliqué piece and attach it to the front of the bib. Tack the top, pink frill to the bottom edge of the bib front. Place on the back of the bib with the right sides facing. Insert the top edge of the apron and sew all the layers together. Fold up the bib pieces and edge stitch the seam on the right side.

6 Bind together the two layers of fabric at the armhole and neckline using the rest of the bias binding strip. Sew the straps to the top of the bib, and the waist ties to the sides.

ROSY WAIST APRON

by Nadia Dalnodar

Measurements **102 x 53cm (40 x 20¾in)**
Templates **Pattern sheet A**

Materials

110 x 10cm (43¼ x 4in) red fabric
120 x 102cm (47¼ x 40in) white fabric with roses
90 x 45cm (35½ x 17¾in) red and white polka dot fabric
60 x 30cm (23½ x 11¾in) white floral fabric
matching thread

Cutting out

A seam allowance of 7.5mm (³/₈ in) is included in
the measurements. The pattern pieces contain no
seam allowance.

Red fabric
2 strips 4 x 105cm (1½ x 41¼in) (ties)

White fabric with roses
2 strips 116 x 15cm (45½ x 6in) (frill)
1 small semi-circular pattern piece, on fold line (pocket)

Red and white polka dot fabric
1 large semi-circular pattern piece, on fold line (apron)

White floral fabric
1 medium semi-circular pattern piece, on fold line (apron)

SEWING

1 To make the ties, join and sew the two red strips along one
short side. Iron this long strip in half lengthwise, and neaten
the raw edges in zigzag stitch. Neaten the other edges in the
same way.

2 To make the frill, join and sew the two strips of white fabric
with roses along one short side. Gather one long side of the
frill to a length of 126cm (49½in). Pin to the curved line of
the large semi-circle with the right sides facing and sew using
zigzag stitch.

3 Pin the semi-circle for the pocket in the middle of the
medium semi-circle 5cm (2in) from the top edge. Sew along
the curved line in a zigzag stitch.

4 For the apron, centre and pin the top edge of the wrong
side of the medium semi-circle to the right side of the top
edge of the large semi-circle, and sew together at a presser
foot's distance.

5 Centre and pin the finished edge of the red waist tie to
the top edge of the apron. Sew all the fabric layers together
along the top edge using zigzag stitch.

BUDDING BAKERS

by Gütermann GmbH

Measurements **48 x 63cm (19 x 24¾in)**
Templates **Pattern sheet A**

Materials

Version 1

70cm (27½in) pink checked fabric
scrap of pink patterned fabric
15cm (6in) tissue paper
15cm (6in) fusible webbing
blue rayon thread
white sewing thread
360cm (11ft 10in) blue bias binding
silicone paper

Version 2

70cm (27½in) turquoise checked fabric
360cm (11ft 10in) brown bias binding
white sewing thread

Version 3

70cm (27½in) fabric with cake pattern
360cm (11ft 10in) pink checked bias binding
white sewing thread

Cutting out

A seam allowance of 7.5mm (³/₈in) is included in
the measurements. The pattern pieces contain no
seam allowance.

Version 1:
Pink checked fabric

1 apron pattern piece, on fold line. Lengthen at bottom by
40cm (15¾in).

Version 2:
Turquoise checked fabric

1 apron pattern piece, on fold line. Lengthen at bottom by
40cm (15¾in).

Version 3:
Fabric with cake pattern

1 apron pattern piece, on fold line. Lengthen at bottom by
40cm (15¾in).

APPLIQUÉ WING

Version 1:

1 Place the pattern piece for the wing on the fold line of a piece
of paper and make a template. Transfer the template to the fusible
webbing and cut out roughly. Iron the fusible webbing onto the
wrong side of the scrap of pink patterned fabric using silicone
paper to protect the iron. Cut out the fabric in the shape of the
wing, and iron it onto the middle of the apron. Back with the
tissue paper and with the blue rayon thread appliqué in a tight
zigzag stitch along the edge before removing the paper.

SEWING

Versions 1-3:

1 To bind the top edge and hem of the apron, place the bias
binding over the edges and edge stitch. To edge the sides, unfold
the lower short side of the bias binding before sewing, iron 1cm
(½in) to the inside and close again.

2 For the ties, halter neck strap and to bind the diagonal edges,
cut a piece of bias binding measuring 198cm (78in). Iron over
the short edges by 1cm (½in). To make the first waist tie, start
at one end and edge stitch the bias binding 48cm (19in) along
the raw edge. After the 48cm (19in), place the bias binding
around the first diagonal edge of the apron and edge stitch. Sew
a further 52cm (20½in) of the bias binding together, also in edge
stitch (this is the halter neck strap), then sew around the second
diagonal edge. Sew the remaining 48cm (19in) down the raw
edge, again in edge stitch, to make the second waist tie.

GARDENING APRON

by Ursula Weppler

Measurements **90 x 72cm (35½ x 28¼in)**
Templates **Pattern sheet A**

Materials

90cm (35½in) coated fabric in turquoise with circles
20cm (7¾in) pink patterned fabric
40cm (15¾in) turquoise patterned fabric
matching thread
4m (13ft) bias binding in pink

Cutting out

A seam allowance of 1cm (½in) is included in
the measurements. The pattern pieces contain no
seam allowance.

Turquoise fabric with circles
1 apron pattern piece, on fold line. Lengthen at bottom by
60cm (23½in).

Pink patterned fabric
2 pocket pattern pieces, on fold line

Turquoise patterned fabric
2 strips 8 x 90cm (3¼ x 35½in) (straps)
2 strips 10 x 90cm (4 x 35½in) (ties)

SEWING

1 Fold the turquoise patterned strips for the straps and waist ties
in half lengthwise. Sew one short side diagonally, then sew along
the long edge. Turn. Fold the seam allowance on the short raw
edge to the inside and edge stitch all around the straps and ties.
Close the opening.

2 For the pocket, place the pattern pieces together with the wrong
sides facing and edge in bias binding. Place the bias binding along
the curved edge and edge stitch in place so that the binding ends up
flush with the fabric. To bind the top edge, cut the bias binding 2cm
(¾in) longer than required and fold over each end by 1cm (½in).
Place over the top edge and edge stitch into place. Place the pocket
in the middle of the apron 35cm (13¾in) from the bottom edge,
and edge stitch along the curved edge.

3 Divide the pocket with two vertical seams 10cm (4in) from
the sides. Bind the apron all around, working from the bottom to
the top. Work the corners as follows: let the bias binding that you
sew on first end flush with the fabric. Fold over the second piece
of binding by 1cm (½in) before sewing. Attach the straps to the
right and left of the top edge. Sew the waist ties to the tops of
the side edges.

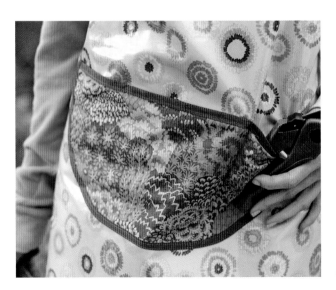

TEA TOWEL APRON

by Heike Ziefuss

Measurements **61 x 54cm (24 x 21¼in)**
Templates **Pattern sheet A**

Materials

2 tea towels in a blue floral pattern
1 tea towel in a blue checked pattern
matching thread
250cm (98½in) white lace, 2cm (¾in) wide
65cm (25½in) white rickrack braid
2 white crochet flowers, 6cm (2¼in) in diameter
6 laundry buttons, 2.5cm (1in) in diameter
water-soluble marker pen or tailor's chalk

Cutting out

A seam allowance of 1cm (½in) is included in the
measurements. The pattern pieces contain no seam
allowance. Before you begin, unpick the hems of the tea
towels and iron them.

Blue floral tea towel
2 pieces 50 x 65cm (19¾ x 25½in) (apron)

Blue checked tea towel
3 strips cut at a 45° angle, 11cm (4¼in) wide, as long
as possible (waist tie)
2 pocket pattern pieces, cut on the diagonal grain

❋❋❋❋❋❋❋❋❋❋❋❋❋❋❋❋❋❋❋❋❋❋❋❋❋

SEWING

1 Neaten one long edge of each of the floral pattern pieces, then sew them together along these edges with the right sides facing. Sew the right side of the rickrack braid to the seam. Make two pleats along the top edge, 5cm and 10.5cm (2in and 4¼in) from the middle respectively. Draw a line 13cm and 15cm (5in and 6in) from the bottom edge. Iron the fabric along the 15cm (6in) line with the wrong sides facing. Pin the top edge of a 100cm (39½in) piece of lace to the 13cm (5in) line and pin the ironed line down over the lace so that 1cm (½in) of the lace remains visible. Edge stitch together. Repeat with two other lines, 8cm and 10cm (3¼in and 4in) from the bottom of the apron. Iron over 1cm (½in) of the two sides of the apron twice and edge stitch into place.

2 To make the waist tie, sew the diagonal strips together to make one strip 200cm (78¾in) long. Iron 1cm (½in) of the two long sides to the wrong side, and iron in half lengthwise with the wrong sides facing. Cut the ends at an angle and iron 1cm (½in) to the inside. Fold the strip 1cm (½in) over the top edge of the apron, starting with the middle of the strip against the middle of the waistband and working to the outside. Edge stitch the strip, attaching the waistband to the top of the apron.

3 Fold over the top edge of the pockets by 1cm (½in) twice and iron on the wrong side. Pin a 19cm (7½in) piece of lace to the back of the top of the pocket with 1cm (½in) of the lace showing, and edge stitch in place. Fold all the other sides 1cm (½in) over to the wrong side twice and iron. Attach the pockets 14cm (5½in) from the top and 10cm (4in) from the side of the apron using edge stitch.

4 Iron over the bottom edge of the apron 1cm (½in) to the wrong side twice and sew. Sew the crochet flowers and buttons to the pockets.

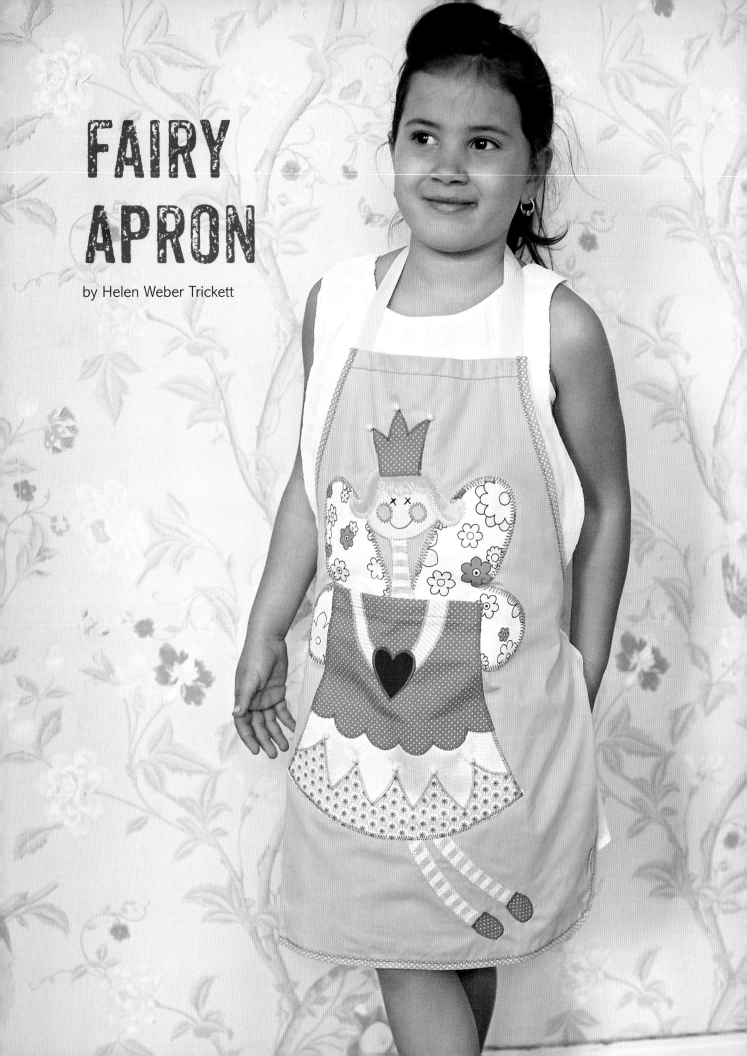

FAIRY APRON

by Helen Weber Trickett

Measurements **56 x 50cm (22 x 19¾in)**
Templates **Pattern sheet A**

Materials

65cm (25½in) pink cotton fabric
65cm (25½in) pale pink and white checked fabric
20cm (7¾in) white fabric with flowers
20cm (7¾in) pink polka dot fabric
25cm (9¾in) white floral fabric
10cm (4in) pale pink satin
fabric scraps in red, yellow (velvet) and pink and white stripes
50cm (19¾in) fusible webbing
machine thread in pale pink and yellow
embroidery thread in brown, purple and pink
200cm (78¾in) bias binding in pale pink with polka dots
130cm (51in) pale pink seam tape, 2cm (¾in) wide
8 pearl-shaped buttons, 5mm (¼in) long
water-soluble marker pen

Cutting out

A seam allowance of 7.5mm (³/₈ in) is included in the measurements. The pattern pieces contain no seam allowance.

Pink cotton fabric
1 apron pattern piece, on fold line, plus 30cm (11¾in) at the bottom (outer apron)

Pale pink and white checked fabric
1 apron pattern piece, on fold line, plus 30cm (11¾in) at the bottom (inner apron)

White floral fabric
1 pocket pattern piece

PREPARATION

Transfer the pattern pieces for the appliqué onto the fusible webbing backing paper and cut out roughly. Iron onto the back of the appropriate fabrics, using the photograph for guidance, and cut out precisely. Remove the backing paper. Cut the seam tape into three pieces of equal length.

APPLIQUÉ

1 Arrange the underskirt, skirt, necklace and heart on the pattern piece for the pocket (see photo) and iron on. Appliqué the individual pieces in zigzag stitch. Sew 5 pearl-shaped buttons onto each tip of the underskirt. Fold over the top of the pocket by 1.5cm (¾in) twice and iron, then sew along the top fold using edge stitch.

2 Centre the pocket in the middle of the outer apron 12.5cm (5in) from the bottom and draw around the outside with the water-soluble marker pen. Use the outline of the pocket to position and iron on the other motifs. Appliqué the wings, neck, head, cheeks, hair, crown and legs using a wide zigzag stitch.

3 Use a normal zigzag stitch for the other items. Place the pocket back on the apron and zigzag along the bottom and up the sides.

4 Embroider the eyes in brown using satin stitch, the mouth in pink or purple using backstitch. Sew a pearl button onto each point of the crown.

SEWING

Place the inside and outside apron pieces together with the right sides facing and sew together at the top. Turn inside out and sew 1.5cm (¾in) from the top. Pin the raw edges together. Place the bias binding over these edges, folding the beginning and end over by 1cm (½in), and secure using zigzag stitch. Hand sew a seam tape loop to the top as the halter neck strap. Sew the other piece to the right and left of the apron as the waist ties.

TASTE OF TRADITION

by Andrea Jahns

Measurements **99 x 86cm (39 x 33¾in)**
Template **Pattern sheet A**

Materials

165 x 140cm (65in x 55in) orange floral fabric
130 x 140cm (51 x 55in) green fabric with flowers
matching thread
2 buttons, 2cm (¾in) in diameter

Cutting out

A seam allowance of 1cm (½in) is included in
the measurements. The pattern pieces contain no
seam allowance.

Orange floral fabric
2 strap frill pattern pieces, on fold line
4 strips 6 x 92cm (2¼ x 36¼in) (straps)
2 pieces 26 x 23cm (10¼in x 9in) (pockets)
2 pieces 132 x 20cm (52 x 7¾in) (hem frill)
2 strips 8 x 75cm (3¼ x 29½in) (waist ties)
1 strips 8 x 90cm (3¼ x 35½in) (waistband)

Green fabric with flowers
1 piece 22 x 55cm (8¾ x 21¾in) (bib)
2 pieces 60 x 46cm (23½ x 18in) (apron sides)
1 piece 60 x 102cm (23½ x 40in) (apron middle)

SEWING

1 To make the strap frills, fold over the short ends and the curved edge by 5mm (¼in) twice and edge stitch in place. Gather the long straight side of the strap frill to 85cm (33½in) (see Basic techniques, page 12). To make the straps, place two pattern pieces together (do this twice) with the right sides facing. Place the strap frill in the middle of them and pin so the frill ends 5cm (2in) before the short sides. The frill will lie between the strap pieces. Sew the straps together along one long edge, catching the frill in the stitches. Fold the remaining edges of the straps to the inside by 1cm (½in) and iron. Fold over the straps so the wrong sides are facing, and edge stitch along the frill edge.

2 Fold the bib in half with the wrong sides facing. Pin the bottoms of the bib sides between the raw strap edges and edge stitch in place. Sew the straps together beyond the bib so they are sewn up on all sides.

3 For the pockets, fold one side over by 1cm (½in) twice (top edge) and edge stitch in place. Iron over the remaining edges to the inside by 1cm (½in), and iron the bottom corners in by 2.5cm (1in) at an angle.

4 Sew the pockets to the middle of the apron, 15cm (6in) from the top (long side) and 8cm (3¼in) from the short side.

5 For the hem frill, sew the pattern pieces together to make one long strip, and gather one of the long sides to 191cm (75in).

6 To make the apron, sew the apron sides to the right and left of the 60cm (23½in) edges of the apron middle. Pin the hem frill to the bottom with the right sides facing, and sew in place.

7 Neaten the seam allowances and fold down the hem frill. Fold over the sides by 1cm (½in) twice and edge stitch into place.

8 Gather the top edge of the apron to 88cm (34¾in) and pin the bib to the middle of it with the wrong sides facing. Sew the waist ties to the right and left of the waistband to make one long strip. Fold all the edges to the inside by 1cm (½in) and iron, then iron the strip in half with the wrong sides facing. Centre the apron (with the bib) 1cm (½in) between the waistband and pin. Sew the waistband along the short and the raw long edge in edge stitch, including the apron and bib in the stitching. Fold up the bib and waistband and sew them together. Make a buttonhole in the waistband above the apron sides, and sew a button to the end of each strap.

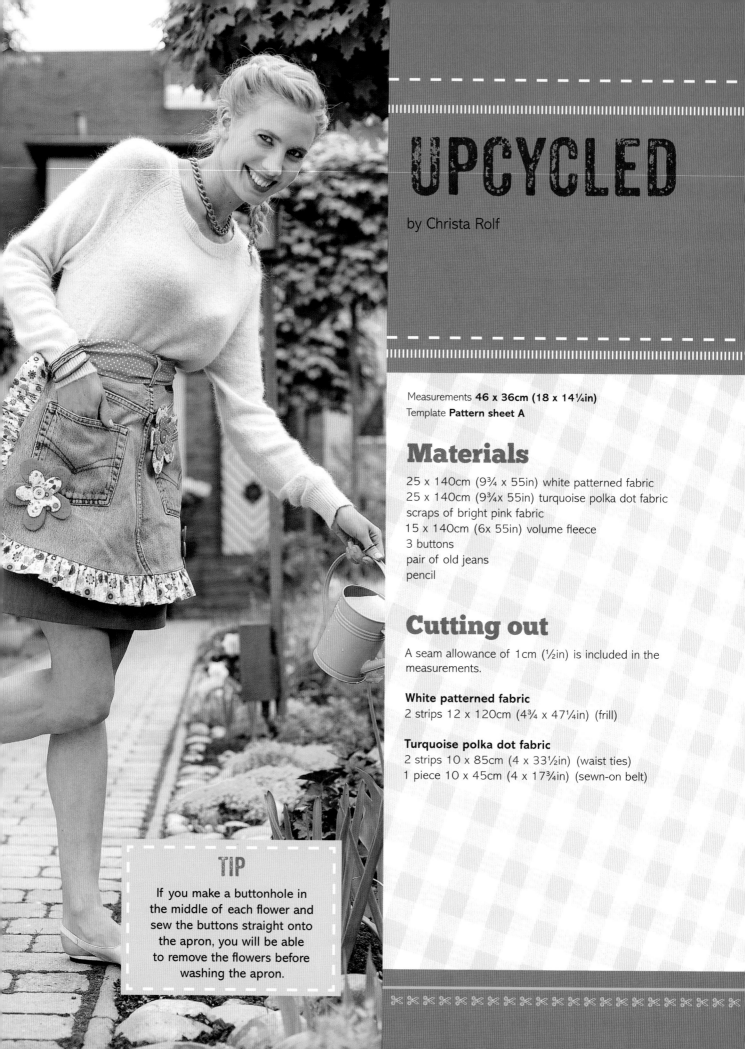

UPCYCLED

by Christa Rolf

Measurements **46 x 36cm (18 x 14¼in)**
Template **Pattern sheet A**

Materials

25 x 140cm (9¾ x 55in) white patterned fabric
25 x 140cm (9¾x 55in) turquoise polka dot fabric
scraps of bright pink fabric
15 x 140cm (6x 55in) volume fleece
3 buttons
pair of old jeans
pencil

Cutting out

A seam allowance of 1cm (½in) is included in the measurements.

White patterned fabric
2 strips 12 x 120cm (4¾ x 47¼in) (frill)

Turquoise polka dot fabric
2 strips 10 x 85cm (4 x 33½in) (waist ties)
1 piece 10 x 45cm (4 x 17¾in) (sewn-on belt)

TIP

If you make a buttonhole in the middle of each flower and sew the buttons straight onto the apron, you will be able to remove the flowers before washing the apron.

SEWING

1 To make the apron, cut the legs off the jeans. Cut off the felled seam on the sides. Undo the seam between the legs a little. Lay the fabric flat and sew the seam up again. Use a dessert plate (approximately 15cm/6in diameter) to round off the two bottom corners.

2 Measure the length required for the frill from one end of the apron to the other.

3 Sew together the two long strips of white patterned fabric to make one long piece. Fold in half lengthwise, and gather to the measured length (see Basic techniques, page 12).

4 To sew the frill to the apron, undo the trouser seam a little at the waistband and tuck the corner of the frill into it. Sew on the frill and neaten the seam using zigzag stitch. Fold the seam allowance to the back, and sew on the right side in edge stitch. Fold the waistband of the trousers back into position and sew.

5 To make the waist ties, fold the two turquoise strips in half lengthwise with the right sides facing. Sew up the seam of one short edge, and leave about 10cm (4in) open at the end of the long edge. Turn the two ties right side out and iron. Fold the seam allowance on the raw seam to the inside and tack if required. Slide both ends of the strips over the waistband and the frill on the outer ends of the waistband and pin as shown. Sew around the waist ties in edge stitch.

6 For the sewn-on belt, fold the remaining turquoise strip over to the wrong side by 5mm (¼in) twice on all sides and edge stitch around the edges. Push the strip through the loops on the jeans and make two tiny pleats at the ends so the belt is as wide as the waistband. Sew on the two ends of the belt by hand.

7 For the appliqué flowers, transfer the template to the back of your chosen fabric. Cut the flower out generously, then place it on another piece of fabric with the right sides facing, and place both of these pieces on a piece of volume fleece.

8 Sew all three layers along the marks. Trim the volume fleece to just before the seam, and trim the fabric seam allowance to 3mm (⅛in). If you want the petals to be especially round and pretty, snip into the seam allowance at small intervals up to the seam.

9 Cut into the top layer of fabric and turn the flower through the slit. This is easier to do if you use the blunt end of a pencil.

10 Sew the flowers on with the buttons. To add variety, you can place one small flower on top of a large one and sew them on together.

TEA TIME

by Doris Trinkl

Measurements **78 x 70cm (30¾ x 27½in)**
Template **Pattern sheet B**

Materials

85cm (33½in) white fabric with patterned design
40cm (15¾in) green and white striped fabric
35cm (13¾in) white lace, 1.5cm (¾in) wide
180cm (71in) pink bias binding with polka dots
matching thread

Cutting out

A seam allowance of 7.5mm (³/₈ in) is included in
the measurements. The pattern pieces contain no
seam allowance.

White patterned fabric
1 apron pattern piece, on fold line. Lengthen at bottom by
50cm (19¾in). Add 2cm (¾in) seam allowance at sides
and on hem; transfer darts to wrong side of fabric.

Green and white striped fabric
2 strips 18 x 75cm (7 x 29½in) (waist ties)

> ## TIP
> A nice patterned fabric featuring
> pots, mugs and rose motifs is ideal
> for the afternoon tea theme of this
> apron project.

SEWING

1 Fold over the hem and sides of the apron by 1cm (½in) twice,
iron and edge stitch. To make the darts, fold the fabric with the
right sides facing along the middle of the dart so the sides meet.
Sew along the mark.

2 Pin the lace to the top of the apron on the right side of the
fabric. Sew on with zigzag stitch, neatening the top edge at the
same time. To make the straps, cut the bias binding into lengths
of 90cm (35½in). Fold the short sides 1cm (½in) to the inside.
Place the bias binding over the curved edge of the armholes,
starting at the side. Fold over the overlapping binding and edge
stitch to secure.

3 Make the waist ties (see Basic techniques, page 12). Place
one end of each at the top of the side of the apron with 3cm
(1¼in) of the tie on the apron. Secure by sewing a rectangle
and its diagonal lines.

ROMANTIC ROSES

by Gütermann GmbH

Measurements **74 x 96cm (29 x 37¾in)**
Template **Pattern sheet B**

Materials

80cm (31½in) white and blue rose pattern fabric
25cm (9¾in) pink and white floral fabric
20cm (7¾in) white and pink daisy leaf fabric
300cm (118in) light blue bias binding
matching thread
35cm (13¾in) narrow pale pink pompom trim
130cm (51in) white bobbin lace, 5mm (¼in) wide

Cutting out

A seam allowance of 7.5mm (³/₈ in) is included in
the measurements. The pattern pieces contain no
seam allowance.

White and blue rose pattern fabric
1 apron pattern piece, on fold line

White and pink daisy leaf fabric
2 pieces 16 x 19cm
(6¼ x 7½in) (pockets)

Pink and white floral fabric
2 strips 8 x 100cm (3¼ x 39½in) (waist ties)
1 strip 7 x 49cm (2¾ x 19¼in) (halter neck strap)
1 strip 7 x 50cm (2¾ x 19¾in) (frill)

SEWING

1 Bind the apron in bias binding, leaving the top. To do this,
unfold the binding and pin it to the edge with the right sides
facing. Sew on the fold. Fold the binding over and position around
the corners, then edge stitch into place.

2 To make the pockets, fold over the top 16cm (6¼in) edges of
the pocket fabric by 1cm (½in) twice and iron, then edge stitch
in place. Trace around a cup to round off the bottom corners
and trim the remaining edges in bias binding. Leave the ends of
the binding to overhang by about 1cm (½in). At the ends, fold
the binding over along the middle ironed line with the right sides
facing, and fold over along the other ironed lines with the wrong
sides facing. Sew together to extend the top of the pocket. Trim
the seam allowance and pin the binding around the edge of the
pocket. Position the pockets evenly on the apron 47cm (18½in)
from the top, with the top corner 9cm (3½in) from the fold line
and the bottom one 7cm (2¾in) from the fold line. Pin the lace
on the bias binding, folding the ends under by 1cm (½in). Sew
along the middle of the lace, including the bias binding in the
stitching, sewing the pocket onto the apron.

3 For the waist ties and halter neck strap, fold the fabric strips
together lengthwise with the right sides facing. Sew along
the long edge. For the waist ties, sew one of the short sides
diagonally. Trim the seam allowances and turn. Fold the seam
allowance of the raw edges to the inside. Edge stitch all the ties.

4 To make the frill, fold the fabric strip in half lengthwise with
the right sides facing, and edge stitch along the short sides. Turn
then iron the fold line. Gather the raw edge to 30cm (11¾in)
(see Basic techniques, page 12). Pin the frill to the top of the
apron with the right sides facing. Pin the ends of the halter
neck strap to the sides. Sew and neaten together. Iron the seam
allowance down. Pin the pompom trim and lace to the top edge
and sew down the middle. Pin the sides of the waist ties behind
the edges of the apron and sew.

MASTERCHEFS

by Emma Curtis and Elizabeth Parnell

Measurements
Mother: 70 x 50cm (27½ x 19¾in);
Child: 50 x 34cm (19¾ x 13½in)
Template **Pattern sheet B**

Materials

80 x 55cm (31½ x 21¾in) beige fabric with small roses
30 x 55cm (11¾ x 21¾in) beige fabric with large roses
55 x 35cm (21¾ x 13¾in) fabric with dog motif
10 x 180cm (4 x 70¾in) pink fabric with roses
matching thread
85cm (33½in) bias binding with polka dots
270cm (106in) ribbon for ties, 2cm (¾in) wide
2 decorative buttons

Cutting out

A seam allowance of 1cm (½in) is included in
the measurements. The pattern pieces contain no
seam allowance.

For the mother's apron: Beige fabric with small roses
1 mother's apron pattern piece, on the fold line. Lengthen
at bottom by 40cm (16in). Add 2cm (¾in) seam
allowance on all sides.

Beige fabric with large roses
1 pocket pattern piece, on fold line. Add 2cm (¾in) seam
allowance to the sides; add 1cm (½in) to the
other edges.

For the child's apron: Fabric with dog motif
1 child's apron pattern piece, on fold line. Lengthen
at bottom by 26cm (10¼in). Add 2cm (¾in) seam
allowance on all sides.

SEWING

1 To make the mother's apron, fold over the top and bottom seams of the pocket and pin (don't worry about the sides as these will be hidden in the hem of the apron).

2 Open the bias binding and align the edge of the binding with the top straight edge of the pocket, right sides together. Pin and sew along the binding crease. Tuck in the corners of the binding and repeat the process on the curved edges of the pocket. Sew the binding over the back of the fabric to complete the pocket.

3 Place your pocket 15cm (6in) up from the bottom of your apron. Flip the pocket over so that the right sides are together, pin in place and sew the pocket base seam on the apron.

4 Once the base of your pocket is attached, pin and sew the top of your pocket to your apron along the seam in the bias binding. Leave the curved edges unstitched.

5 Find the middle line of your pocket and sew a vertical line from the top to the bottom to create two pocket sections.

6 Cut 50cm (19¾in) of ribbon for your neck loop. Fold over a 1cm (½in) hem at the top of your apron. Place your ribbon 3cm (1¼in) in from each edge of the apron and fold over a 1cm (½in) hem again, enclosing your ribbon. Pin and sew the hem.

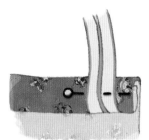

7 Pin and sew a double hem (where you fold, then fold again so no raw edges are showing) on each of the side curved edges of your apron.

8 Pin and sew a double hem down the remaining raw edges, folding in a 50cm (19¾in) piece of ribbon at each side (as done previously on the neck loop), about 1cm (½in) down from the curved edges.

9 To finish, fold, pin and sew a double hem along the bottom of your apron.

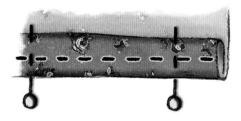

10 To make the child's apron, hem the apron, cut out and attach the neck loop ribbon (about 40cm or 15¾in) as in Step 6. Hem both scoops of the apron and add a cute frill by gathering the strip of pink fabric with roses (see Basic techniques, page 12). Add ribbon for waist ties (about 40cm or 15¾in for each side).

SPICK & SPAN

by Sylvia Ferron

Measurements **86 x 72cm (34 x 28¼in)**
Template **Pattern sheet B**

Materials

90cm (35½in) blue striped cotton fabric
matching thread
240cm (94½in) dark blue woven tape, 3cm (1¼in) wide
3 laundry buttons, 1.7cm (¾in) in diameter
1 dark blue hand towel, 30 x 50cm (11¾ x 19¾in)
water-soluble marker pen

Cutting out

A seam allowance of 7.5mm (³/₈in) is included in
the measurements. The pattern pieces contain no
seam allowance.

Blue striped cotton fabric
1 apron pattern piece, on fold line. Lengthen at bottom
by 60cm (23½in). Add 2cm (¾in) seam allowance on
all sides.
1 piece 9.5 x 37.5cm (3¾ x 14¾in) (button placket)

Woven tape
2 pieces 50cm (19¾in) (straps)
2 pieces 70cm (27½in) (waist ties)

TIP
A convenient feature of
this apron is the button-on
placket. Use this to attach a
hand towel for drying.

SEWING

1 For the apron, fold over 1cm (½in) twice on the armholes and
hem, iron, then edge stitch. Fold over one short side of each piece
of woven tape by 5mm (¼in) twice and edge stitch. To attach
the straps, place the raw short edges to the right and left of the
top of the apron. Fold over both the top edge and the straps by
1cm (½in) twice and edge stitch. Attach the waist ties to the side
edges in the same way.

2 Fold the fabric piece for the button placket in half lengthwise
with the wrong sides facing, sew up the short sides then turn.
Make three buttonholes (see buttonhole diagram on Pattern
sheet B). Draw a 36cm (14¼in) line across the middle of the
right side of the apron 27.5cm (11in) from the top edge. Place
the raw edge of the button placket against this line with the right
sides facing and sew at a presser foot's distance. Iron over to
the bottom and sew at a presser foot's distance. Sew the three
buttons 12cm (4¾in) apart on one short side of the towel. Button
to the button placket.

DIRNDL
APRON

by Stefanie Riediger

Measurements **94 x 34cm (37 x 13½in)**

Materials

140cm (55in) purple striped fabric, 160cm (63in) wide
matching thread
35cm (13¾in) fusible webbing/interfacing
125cm (49¼in) elastic ruffle tape, 5cm (2in) wide

Cutting out

A seam allowance of 1cm (½in) is included in
the measurements.

Purple striped fabric
2 strips 140 x 10cm (55 x 4in) (waist ties)
1 strip 72 x 7cm (28¼ x 2¾in) (waistband)
1 piece 100 x 125cm (39½ x 49in) (apron)

SEWING

1 To make the waist ties, fold the fabric strips in half lengthwise
and angle one short end at 45°. Sew along the long and the angled
edges, turn and iron.

2 Iron the fusible webbing/interfacing onto the middle of the
waistband, and fold the two short sides 1cm (½in) to the inside.
Tack the stretchy ruffle tape evenly to the top edge of the apron.
Sew to the fabric between the elastic threads, then pull the elastic
threads to gather to 38cm (15in). Fold over the side edges by 1cm
(½in) twice and edge stitch.

3 Sew the waistband along the top apron edge with right sides
facing. Fold up, then fold in half lengthwise with the wrong sides
facing and fold over the seam allowances to the inside. Push the raw
edges of the waist ties between the waistband layers, and arrange
the excess fabric in a pleat in the middle.

4 Edge stitch the waistband on all sides. Fold over the hem of the
apron by 4cm (1½in) twice and edge stitch to finish.

NEWSPRINT APRON

Measurements **83 x 40cm (32¾ x 15¾in)**
Template **Pattern sheet A**

Materials

90cm (35½in) fabric with newspaper print
35cm (13¾in) green fabric with a dark pattern
10cm (4in) brown patterned fabric
20cm (7¾in) green patterned fabric
20cm (7¾in) turquoise patterned fabric
20cm (7¾in) brightly patterned fabric matching threads

Cutting out

A seam allowance of 5mm (¼in) is included in the measurements. The pattern pieces also include a seam allowance.

Green fabric with a dark pattern
2 strips 5 x 56cm (2 x 22in) (straps)
3 strips 7.5 x 56cm (3 x 22in) (ties)

Fabric with newspaper print
2 pieces 30.5 x 25cm (12 x 9¾in) (apron top)
1 piece 56 x 56cm (22 x 22in) (apron skirt)

Brown patterned fabric
2 border pattern pieces, on fold line

Green patterned fabric
1 strip 15 x 106.5cm (6 x 42in) (frill)

Turquoise patterned fabric
1 strip 15 x 106.5cm 6 x 42in) (frill)

Brightly patterned fabric
1 strip 15 x 106.5cm (6 x 42in) (frill)

SEWING

1 Fold over to the wrong side one short side of each of the strap pieces by 5mm (¼in) and iron. Make up the straps (see Basic techniques, page 12). To make the front and back of the apron top, pin one border piece to the short side of each apron top piece, right sides facing, and sew 5mm (¼in) from the edge. Centre and pin the raw edge of the straps centrally to an arch 4cm (1½in) from the side.

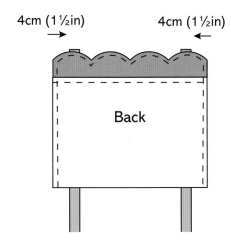

4cm (1½in)   4cm (1½in)

Back

2 Place the front and back together with the right sides facing and sew around as far as the bottom edge. Snip into the seam allowance on the curves and cut off the corners at an angle. Turn.

3 To make the apron skirt, turn the edge 5mm (¼in) to the wrong side twice on three sides of the pattern piece, iron and edge stitch. Gather the raw top edge to 40cm (16in) (see Basic techniques, page 12). With the wrong sides facing, tack the prepared apron top centrally to the top edge of the skirt.

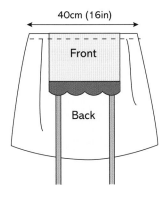

40cm (16in)

Front

Back

4 Sew together the three sections for the waistband and ties in one long strip. Iron all the edges to the wrong side by 5mm (¼in) then iron the strip in half lengthwise. Place the waistband centrally over the seam allowances of the apron top and skirt. Edge stitch the band close to the raw edges, including the apron in the sewing.

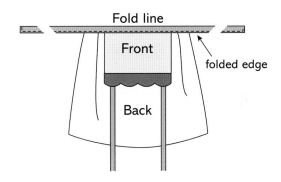

Fold line

Front

Back

folded edge

5 Unfold the apron top and pin the waistband to it then sew together along the top edge.

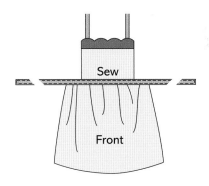

Sew

Front

6 To make the three frills, iron the short sides and one long side 5mm (¼in) to the wrong side twice and edge stitch. Iron 15mm (¾in) of the raw edges to the inside and gather to 53.5cm (21in) (see Basic techniques, page 12). Sew the frills 10cm (4in), 15cm (6in) and 20cm (7¾in) respectively from the bottom edge of the skirt, with the wrong side of the frill against the right side of the apron. Start with the bottom frill.

SMARTLY RUFFLED

by Hannelore Duschl

Measurements **100 x 58cm (39½ x 23in)**
Templates **Pattern sheet B**

Materials

200 x 140cm (78¾ x 55in) red and white fabric
matching thread
100cm (39½in) white piping
2 white buttons, 2cm (¾in) in diameter

Cutting out

A seam allowance of 1cm (½in) is included in
the measurements. The pattern pieces contain no
seam allowance.

Red and white fabric
2 pieces 5 x 17cm (2 x 6¾ in) (pocket pad)
2 pieces 17 x 19.5cm (6¾ x 7¾in) (pocket)
2 strips 85 x 12cm (33½ x 4¾in) (straps)
2 strap frill pattern pieces, 70cm (27½in) long on raw
straight edge
1 bib (front) pattern piece, on fold line
2 bib (side) pattern pieces
1 piece 32 x 30cm (12½ x 11¾in) (bib pad)
1 strip 152 x 22cm (60 x 8¾in) (skirt frill)
1 piece 85 x 52cm (33½ x 20½in) (skirt)
2 waist ties pattern pieces, lengthen by 30cm (11¾in)
on raw edge
2 strips 63 x 5cm (25 x 2in) (waistband)

SEWING

1 To make the pockets, line up the pad and pocket pieces on their 17cm (6¾in) edges, right sides facing. Work in a 17cm (6¾in) piece of piping. Place the piping between the two fabric pieces (with the cord on the inside) and sew in with the seam using the zip foot on your machine. Fold the pad piece down; the piping finishes the top edge. On the raw sides, iron over 1cm (½in) to the inside. Sew the pockets onto the skirt at a distance of 13cm (5in) from the side and 11.5cm (4½in) from the top.

2 For the straps, fold the long edges and one short edge 1cm (½in) to the inside and iron. Fold the straps in half lengthwise with the wrong sides facing and iron.

3 Neaten the strap frills on the curved side, fold over 1cm (½in) and sew on. Gather the long straight sides to 56cm (22in) (see Basic techniques, page 12).

4 To make the bib, sew the bib sides to the right and left of the bib front, sewing in a 31cm (12¼in) piece of piping as you work. Fold over the side edges of the bib and bib pad 1cm (½in) to the wrong side and iron. Place the bib and pad together with the right sides facing. Insert the straps at the top with the raw short side and the fold line on the inside. Sew the fabrics together along the top, starting and ending 1cm (½in) from the sides. Insert the strap frill between the bib and pad on the side or into the raw outer edge of the straps, starting at the bottom edge of the bib. Edge stitch up the side of the bib and straps and the short strap end.

5 Neaten the skirt frill on all sides, fold over by 1cm (½in) along one long side and sew. Gather the other long side to 85cm (33½in) and sew to the bottom part of the skirt. Fold six 4cm (1½in) pleats at the top of the skirt and pin; the skirt should be 61cm (24in) wide. Fold the skirt over by 1cm (½in) at the sides and sew.

6 Fold over the long sides and the wider short side of the waist ties by 5mm (¼in) twice and sew. Bring the outer corners on the wide short edge in to the middle to make a point and secure with a few stitches.

7 For the waistband, iron one long side 1cm (½in) to the inside on both pieces. Place the pieces together with the right sides facing, and insert the skirt between them. The top edge of the skirt should be flush with the raw waistband edges. Put the raw short edges of the waist ties between the short sides of the waistband pieces so that one side of the waist ties is flush with the folded waistband. Sew the waistband to the short side and along the raw long edge. Fold the waistband up and put out the waist ties.

8 Insert the bib centrally between the waistband pieces. Edge stitch the top waistband, including the bib in the sewing. Work a vertical buttonhole on the waistband between the side edges of the skirt. Hold the apron against yourself to determine the position of the button on the front of the straps, and sew the buttons on as close to the edge as you can.

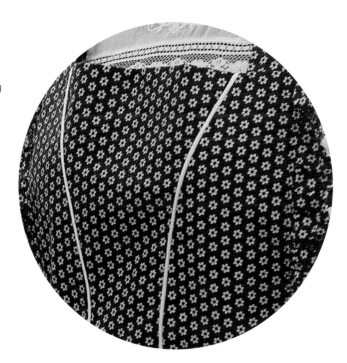

GOOD ENOUGH TO EAT

by Christa Rolf

Measurements **46 x 36cm (18 x 14¼in)**

Materials

35cm (13¾in) fabric with cupcakes
70cm (27½in) border fabric with flowers
25cm (9¾in) blue polka dot fabric
matching threads

Cutting out

A seam allowance of 7.5mm ($^3/_8$ in) is included in
the measurements.

Fabric with cupcakes
1 piece 40 x 30cm (16 x 11¾in) (apron)

Blue polka dots fabric
2 strips 10 x 110cm (4 x 43¼in) (frill)

Border fabric
3 strips 9 x 65cm (3½ x 25½in) (waistband and ties) –
make sure that the pattern runs across the three strips.

SEWING

1 For the apron, use a dinner plate (approximately 20cm or 7¾in
diameter) to round off the two bottom corners.

2 For the frill, sew the two fabric strips together to make one long
length, then trim it to 180cm (71in). Fold the strip in half lengthwise
and gather to the length of the circumference of the sides and
bottom of the apron (see Basic techniques, page 12). Sew the frill
onto the apron and neaten with zigzag stitch.

3 To make the waistband and ties, sew the three strips together
to make one long piece. Pin the waistband to the apron, right sides
facing, and with the edges aligned (make sure that the apron is
positioned centrally), and sew on. Fold the two overlapping ends of
the waistband in half with the right sides facing and angle the ends.
Sew together until just before the edge of the apron. Turn out and
iron the ties, and iron the fold (top edge) along the entire length of
the waistband. Fold the seam allowance for the apron to the inside
and pin to the apron. Edge stitch the waistband on all sides, sewing it
to the inside of the apron.

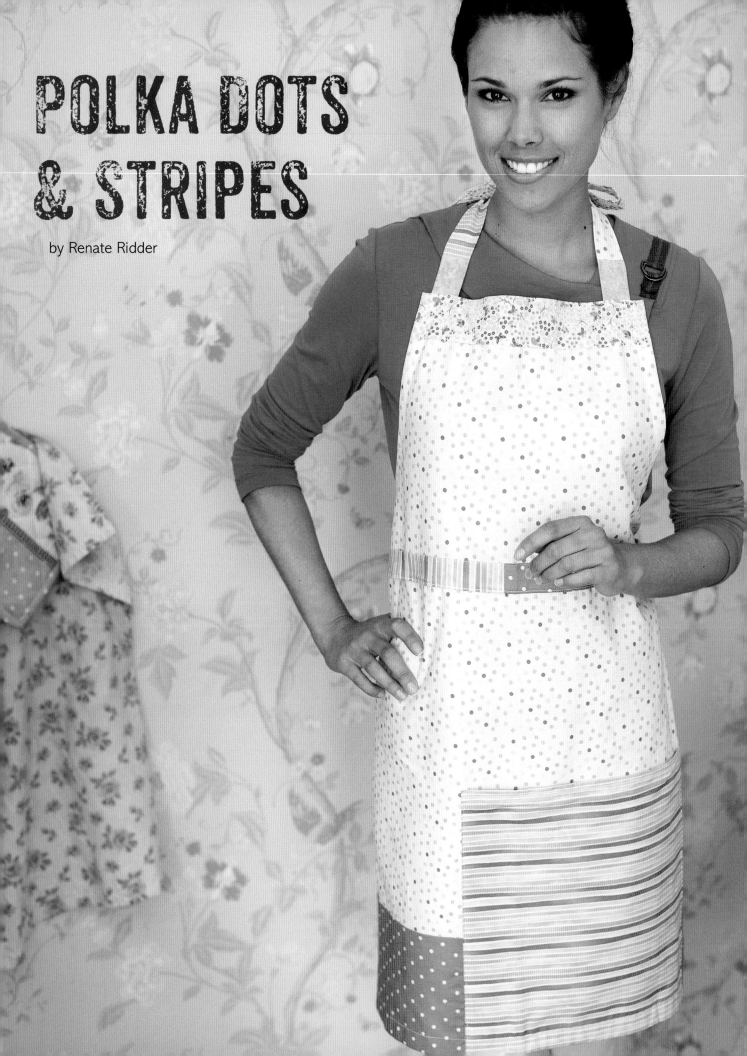

POLKA DOTS & STRIPES

by Renate Ridder

Measurements **83 x 68cm (32¾ x 26¾in)**
Templates **Pattern sheet A**

Materials

100m (39½in) white polka
dot fabric
30cm (11¾in) striped fabric
30cm (11¾in) pink and white polka dot fabric
10cm (4in) turquoise fabric
20cm (7¾in) patterned fabric
matching threads
pencil

Cutting out

A seam allowance of 7.5mm (³/₈ in) is included
in the measurements. The pattern pieces contain no
seam allowance.

White polka dot fabric
1 apron pattern piece, on fold line. Lengthen at bottom by
52cm (20½in). Add 2cm (¾in) seam allowance to the
sides, and 7.5mm (³/₈ in) elsewhere.
1 piece 3.5 x 72cm (1½ x 28¼in) (hem padding)
1 strip 7.5cm (3in) wide (waist ties)
2 diagonal strips 3.5 x 40cm (1½ x 16in) (pad for
curved edge)

Striped fabric
1 piece 30 x 62cm (11¾ x 24½in) (pocket)
cut the remainder into strips 7.5cm (3in) wide
(waist ties)

Pink and white polka dot fabric
1 piece 15.5 x 72cm (6 x 28¼in) (hem facing)
1 strip 7.5cm (3in) wide (waist ties)

Turquoise fabric
1 strip 7.5cm (3in) wide (waist ties)

Patterned fabric
1 strip 7.5cm (3in) wide (waist ties)
1 strip 6.5 x 30cm (2½ x 11¾in) wide (facing at top)

SEWING

1 For the ties, cut the five strips into sections of between 15cm and
25cm (6in and 9¾in) long. Assemble them as you like then sew
together to make one strip 240cm (94½in) long (waistband and
ties) and two strips 70cm (27½in) long (straps). Iron over the seam
allowance on all sides of the waistband, and only the long ones and
one short one on the straps. Fold the strips in half with the wrong
sides facing, and edge stitch along the folded edges.

2 For the pocket, fold the fabric piece in half crossways with the
right sides facing (the fold line is at the top) and sew up the sides.
Turn and sew the fold at a presser foot's distance from the edge.

3 For the hem facing, draw a pencil line 14cm (5½in) from the
bottom edge of the apron on the right side. Place the facing on the
line from the top, right sides facing, then sew at a presser foot's
distance and fold down. Place the pocket on the hem 12.5cm (5in)
from the right edge and sew along both sides. To add definition,
place the hem padding on the bottom edge of the hem with the right
sides facing and sew. Fold to the inside then fold the seam allowance
to the inside, and edge stitch.

4 For the top facing, draw a line 5cm (2in) from the top edge as
for the hem facing. Position the top facing with its top edge along
the line, right sides facing, and sew. Fold over and iron all the seam
allowances on the top edge to the inside. Insert the straps 1.5cm
(¾in) from the side with the raw edge. Edge stitch the top edge,
including the straps in the stitching. At the curves, place
the diagonal strips on the apron with the right sides facing and
sew. Fold to the inside, fold the seam allowance to the inside, and
edge stitch.

5 Iron over the side edges by 1cm (½in) twice and sew. Pin the
waistband centrally onto the apron below the curves (with the fold at
the top). Sew a rectangle on the two sides and in the middle of the
band to secure.

ONE FOR
THE BOYS

Measurements **73 x 76cm (28¾ x 30in)**
Templates **Pattern sheet B**

Materials

80cm (31½in) black fabric
30cm (11¾in) fabric with newspaper print
50cm (19¾in) black and white checked fabric
30cm (11¾in) black fabric with fried eggs
matching thread

Cutting out

A seam allowance of 1cm (½in) is included in
the measurements. The pattern pieces contain no
seam allowance.

Black fabric
1 piece 55 x 80cm (21¾ x 31½in) (apron skirt)
2 strips 6 x 90cm
(2¼ x 35½in) (waistband)

Fabric with newspaper print
1 apron top pattern piece, on fold line

Black and white checked fabric
1 strip 6 x 60 (2¼ x 23½in) (halter neck strap)
2 pieces 54 x 22cm
(21¼ x 8¾in) (large pocket)

Black fabric with fried eggs
2 pieces 20 x 30cm
(7¾ x 11¾in) (small pocket)

SEWING

1 To make the ties and straps, fold the fabric pieces in half lengthwise with right sides facing, and sew along the long sides. Turn through.

2 To make the large and small pockets, place the two pattern pieces together with right sides facing, sew up three sides and turn.

3 Iron the ties and pockets and edge stitch on all sides, folding the raw edges on the short sides of the ties and turning openings of the pockets to the inside. Fold over the apron top and skirt by 1cm (½in) twice on all sides and edge stitch. Pin the halter neck strap ends to the right and left of the upper part of the apron. Sew a rectangle with diagonal lines to attach each end to the apron.

4 Place the apron top centrally over the skirt, overlapping slightly, and secure with two parallel seams. Sew the smaller pocket centrally to the top, 10cm (4in) from the top edge, and the large pocket centrally 12cm (4¾in) below the waistband at the sides and bottom edge. If you wish, sew a vertical line in the small pocket to make two smaller pockets as shown in the photograph.

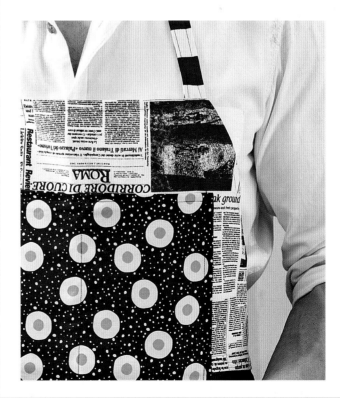

PIPPI LONGSTOCKING APRON

Measurements
For a child: height 100cm (39½in), chest 60cm (23½in)
Templates **Pattern sheet B**

Materials

50cm (19¾in) pink patterned fabric
50cm (19¾in) pink polka dot fabric
50cm (19¾in) white fabric with flowers
40cm (16in) white fabric with pink flowers
matching thread
160cm (63in) green crochet edging, 2.5cm (1in) wide
2 pink and green crocheted flowers, 2.5cm (1in)
in diameter

Cutting out

A seam allowance of 1cm (½in) is included in
the measurements. The pattern pieces contain no
seam allowance.

Pink patterned fabric
1 apron front pattern piece, on fold line (no seam
allowance for neckline or armholes)

Pink polka dot fabric
1 apron back pattern piece (no seam allowance for
armholes and neckline from shoulder to start of
crochet trim)

White fabric with flowers
1 apron back pattern piece, mirror image (seam
allowance as above)

White fabric with pink flowers
4 diagonal strips 4cm (1½in) wide cut against the grain
(bias binding for neck and armholes)

SEWING

1 To make the apron, place the front and back pieces together at the sides, right sides facing, and sew up. Neaten the seam allowances. Arrange the shoulder edges of the back pieces on the shoulder edges of the front pieces so that the back pieces are crossed over. Sew the shoulders together and neaten. Neaten the hem and iron the seam allowance to the inside. Pin the crochet edging between the marks on the wrong side of the hem so that the curved edge is visible from the right side and edge stitch.

2 For the trim, sew the diagonal strips together to make one long strip. Fold in half lengthwise and iron. Open out, then fold the two long sides to the middle and fold over again. Iron in the folds. Place the trim around the edges of the neckline and armholes, pinning the ends of the crochet edging to the short sides between the trim, and edge stitch the binding strips. Sew on the crochet flowers at the cross-over point between the crochet edging and the diagonal strip. You can use ready-made crochet edging and flowers or make your own.

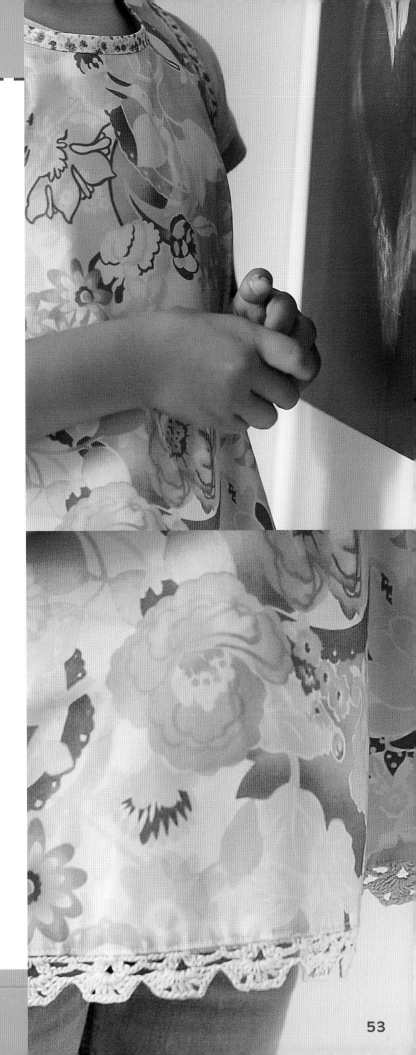

FROM THE HEART

by Ursula Weppler

Measurements **80 x 66cm (31½ x 26in)**
Templates **Pattern sheet B**

Materials

60cm (23½in) purple patterned fabric
40cm (16in) bright pink and white polka dot fabric
40cm (16in) pink and white striped fabric
150cm (59in) bright pink bias binding
matching thread
19 white buttons, 1.5cm (¾in) in diameter

Cutting out

A seam allowance of 1cm (½in) is included in
the measurements. The pattern pieces contain no
seam allowance.

Pink and white striped fabric
2 strips 10 x 98cm (4 x 38½in) (waistband and ties)
2 strips 8 x 77cm (3¼ x 30¼in) (straps)

Purple patterned fabric
1 apron pattern piece, on fold line

Bright pink and white polka dot fabric
2 heart bib pattern pieces, on fold line
4 heart-shaped pocket pattern pieces

SEWING

1 To make the waistband and ties, sew both the strips together to make one long piece. Iron all the sides of the waistband and straps to the wrong side by 1cm (½in). Fold the strips in half lengthwise with the wrong sides facing and iron. Edge stitch the straps on all sides.

2 Make two pockets and turn right side out (see Basic techniques, page 12). Position the pockets 5cm (2in) from the top and 9cm (3½in) from the centre, and edge stitch just below the marks printed on the pattern.

3 Cover the curved bottom of the apron skirt by placing the folded bias binding along it and edge stitching in place. Pin the top of the apron centrally 1cm (½in) between the waistband pieces. Edge stitch the waistband on all sides, including the apron in the stitching.

4 Pin the straps to the bib with right sides facing and the straps on the inside. Turn out the pieces for the bib, making sure that the straps are taken up between the marks. Close the opening and edge stitch all around. Place the bib centrally on top of the apron with 7cm (2¾in) of the bottom of the heart overlapping the top of the apron skirt. Edge stitch the overlapping part of the bib to the apron. Arrange the 19 buttons evenly around the bib and sew in place.

SWEET TEMPTATION

by Ingrid Weber

Measurements **85 x 59cm (33½ x 23¼in)**
Templates **Pattern sheet A**

Materials

90cm (35½in) cupcake fabric in mint
25cm (9¾in) beige floral fabric
30cm (11¾in) multicoloured striped fabric
20cm (7¾in) fabric with sweet jar motif
15cm (6in) fusible webbing
matching thread
130cm (51in) pale pink bias binding

Cutting out

A seam allowance of 75mm ($^3/_8$ in) is included in the measurements. The pattern pieces contain no seam allowance.

Cupcake fabric in mint
1 apron pattern piece, on fold line. Lengthen at bottom by 55cm (23¾in). Add 3cm (1¼in) top and sides, and 5cm (2in) at bottom and on curves without seam allowances.

Beige floral fabric
1 piece 40.5 x 23.5cm (16 x 9¼in) (pocket)

Multi-coloured striped fabric
2 strips 83 x 8cm (32¾ x 3 ¼in) (waistband and ties)
1 strip 55 x 10cm (21¾ x 4in) (halter neck strap)

Fusible webbing
1 piece 11 x 14cm (4¼ x 5½in)

PREPARATION

Iron the fusible webbing onto the back of the sweet jar fabric so it sits behind one of the jars. Cut out the sweet jar precisely. Remove the backing paper.

SEWING

1 Trim the curved edges of the apron in bias binding by edge stitching it in place. Fold the top edge and sides over to the wrong side by 1.5cm (¾in) twice and edge stitch. Fold the hem over by 2.5cm (1in) twice and edge stitch.

2 Fold the short sides of the waist ties and the halter neck strap to the inside by 1cm (½in) and iron. Sew the ties (see Basic techniques, page 12), edge stitching the short sides as well. Sew the halter neck strap to the left and right of the top edge. Sew the waist ties to the sides.

3 To make the pocket, trim one long side (top edge) with bias binding. Fold the other sides to the inside by 7.5mm ($^3/_8$ in) twice and iron. Place the pocket in the middle of the apron 29cm (11½in) from the top, and edge stitch along the bottom and the two sides. Sew a vertical line down the middle of the pocket to divide it. Position the sweet jar motif on the bottom right of the pocket and iron on.

NEON BRIGHT

by Ursula Weppler

Measurements **81 x 72cm (32 x 28¼in)**
Templates **Pattern sheet A**

Materials

65cm (25½in) green and white polka dot fabric
65cm (25½in) white fabric with hearts
40cm (15¾in) orange fabric, thread in neon green, neon
orange, neon yellow and neon pink
1 green button, 4cm (1½in) in diameter
1 overall button, 2cm (¾in) in diameter
water-soluble marker

Cutting out

A seam allowance of 1cm (½in) is included in
the measurements.

Green and white polka dot fabric
1 piece 58 x 58cm (23 x 23in) (apron square 1)

White fabric with hearts
1 piece 58 x 58cm (23 x 23in) (apron square 2)

Orange fabric
2 strips 8 x 95cm (3¼ x 37½in) (straps)
2 strips 10 x 95cm (4 x 37½in) (waist ties)

SEWING

1 Fold the waist ties and straps in half lengthwise with right sides facing. Sew diagonally across one short side, then sew together along the long side. Turn. Edge stitch in neon yellow (top thread) and neon orange (bottom thread). Pin the straps and waist ties to apron square 1 with the raw edge to the outside and right sides facing (see diagram on Pattern sheet A). Pin apron square 2 to the first one with the right sides facing and sew before turning through. Edge stitch in neon green (top thread) and neon pink (bottom thread). Sew a line between the shoulder straps on the top point (see photo).

2 To position the buttonhole, fold down the top point of the square so the fold line is between the top edges of the waist ties. Mark the beginning and end of the buttonhole (for the overall button) on the fold with the water-soluble marker. The starting point is 13cm (5in) from the edge. Sew the buttonhole. Sew the green button to the overall button, then push the smaller button through the buttonhole.

OWL APRON

by Ingrid Perra

Measurements **70 x 85cm (27½ x 33½in)**
Templates **Pattern sheet B**

Materials

100 x 100cm (39½ x 39½in) pink and white polka
dot fabric
30 x 140cm (11¾ x 55in) green checked fabric
80 x 110cm (31½ x 43¼in) multi-coloured fabric
15 x 10cm (6 x 4in) lilac fabric with stars
10 x 10cm (4 x 4in) white fabric
10 x 10cm (4 x 4in) fusible volume fleece
10 x 10cm (4 x 4in) embroidery fleece
scraps of fusible volume fleece
matching threads
2 black buttons, 2cm (¾in) diameter

Cutting out

A seam allowance of 7.5mm (³/₈ in) is included in
the measurements. The pattern pieces contain no
seam allowance.

Pink and white polka dot fabric
1 apron top pattern piece. Lengthen at bottom by 35cm
(13¾in). Add 4cm (1½in) at top edge, plus seam
allowance; add 2cm (¾in) to other edges.
2 strips 16 x 64cm (6¼ x 25¼in) (straps)

Multicoloured fabric
1 apron bottom pattern piece. Lengthen at the bottom by
50cm (19¾in), no seam allowance; add 2cm (¾in) to
other edges.

Green checked fabric
4 ear pattern pieces
2 strips 8 x 75cm (3¼ x 29½in) (waist ties)
1 piece 10 x 74cm (4 x 29in) (spectacles)

Lilac fabric with stars
2 beak pattern pieces

Scraps of fusible volume fleece
3 ears/beak pattern pieces

PREPARATION

Transfer the templates for the spectacles (1) and eyes (2) to the
backing paper of the scraps of fusible webbing. Cut out roughly, and
iron onto the backs of the various fabrics. Use the photo for guidance.
Cut out precisely and remove the backing paper.

SEWING

1 For the beak, iron the fusible volume fleece onto the back of one
piece of fabric. Place the other piece on top with the right sides
facing and sew along the long edge. Leave the short side open for
turning. Turn. Make the ears in the same way, but here sew up the
opening left for turning by hand.

2 Pin the spectacles to the middle of the apron top, 16cm (6¼in)
from the top edge. Slide the beak under the bottom edge, and iron
on the spectacles. Sew along all sides with a tight zigzag stitch.

3 Iron the eyes onto the relevant parts of the spectacles, and
appliqué in the same way. Position the buttons on the eyes and
sew on.

4 To make the straps, fold over one short side by 1cm (½in) and
sew (see Basic techniques, page 12). Fold over the long sides of the
waist ties by 1cm (½in) twice and sew. On the short sides, fold the
corners to the middle to make a point. Edge stitch to secure.

5 For the apron, fold over the fabric 1cm (½in) twice along the
curved sides of the top and bottom parts, and the hem of the upper
part of the apron and sew.

6 Fold over the seam allowances on the long sides of the apron top.
Edge stitch the bottom hem.

7 Pin the bottom part of the apron to the top part, wrong side on
right, with 20.5cm (8in) space between the top hems. Sew together
along the hem of the top apron part. Sew a triangle in the point of
the bottom section of the apron to join together the apron halves. Pin
the straight, short side of the waist ties to the sides 1.5cm (¾in)
from the top. Fold all the layers over by 1cm (½in) twice at the sides
and sew.

8 Fold over the top edge by 2cm (¾in) twice. Pin the straps 1cm
(½in) from the side with the raw edge and sew along the tuck-in.
Fold the straps up; the tuck-in will flip down to the front. Pin the ears
to the front sides of the tuck-in, and include the straps – folded up –
when you sew them on.

THE TWO OF US

by Christa Rolf

Measurements
Child's apron: 57 x 44cm (22½ x 17¼in)
Adult's apron: 97 x 70cm (38¼ x 27½in)
Templates **Pattern sheet A**

Materials

scraps of white fabric
15cm (6in) white and red polka dot fabric
15cm (6in) fusible webbing
black and white thread
1 Ikea 'Julkul' apron for adults
1 Ikea 'Julkul' apron for children
70cm (27½in) red and white lace
2 red buttons
water-soluble marker

Cutting out

A seam allowance of 7.5mm (³⁄₈ in) is included in
the measurements. The appliqué pieces contain no
seam allowance.

Scraps of white fabric
1 circle 7cm (2¾in) in diameter (yo-yo for the child's apron)
1 circle 5cm (2in) in diameter (yo-yo for the adult's apron)

PREPARATION

Transfer the patterns for the wording and flower to fusible
webbing and cut out generously. Iron onto the back of the white
and red polka dot fabric. Cut out precisely along the outline and
remove the backing paper from the fusible webbing. Iron the
word 'MAMA' onto the adult's apron and the flower onto the
child's apron.

SEWING

1 For the appliqué, sew the letters 2mm (¹⁄₁₀in) from the outer
edge using a small stitch (stitch length 1.5). Draw the lines onto
the flower petals in water-soluble marker, then sew along them
in black thread. Make two yo-yos out of the fabric circles (see
Basic techniques, page 12) and sew each one on with a button.
The larger yo-yo goes in the middle of the flower, the smaller
one at the tip of the 'A' of 'MAMA'.

2 Sew the lace along the top edge of the adult apron, leaving
a little overlapping at the ends. Fold the lace to the back and
sew on by hand.

3 On the child's apron, separate a short section of the top
edge of the pocket from the apron. Sew the lace to this edge,
and sew the pocket back on again.